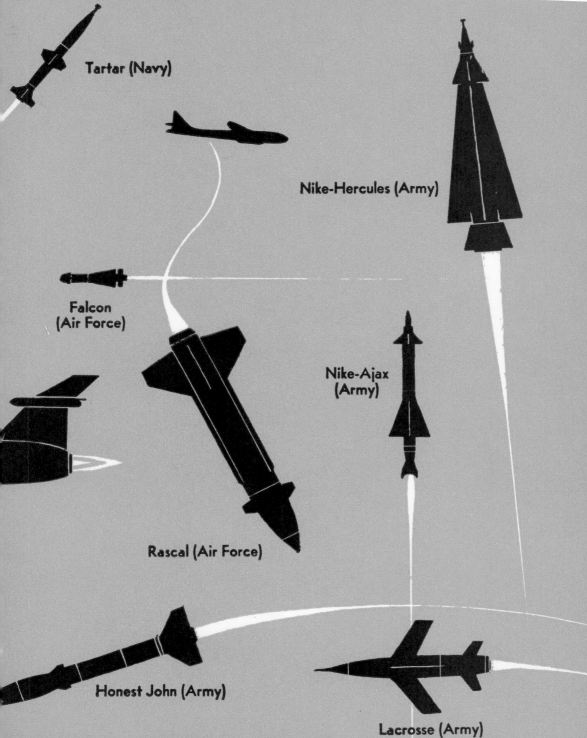

Tartar (Navy)

Nike-Hercules (Army)

Falcon
(Air Force)

Nike-Ajax
(Army)

Rascal (Air Force)

Honest John (Army)

Lacrosse (Army)

All About Rockets and Jets

All About Rockets and Jets

allabout
books

By Fletcher Pratt

Illustrated by Jack Coggins

RANDOM HOUSE
NEW YORK

SECOND EDITION

THIRD PRINTING

Contents

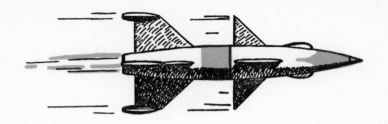

Foreword

Unfortunately most people will never see the take-off of a big rocket except in the newsreels and on television. The reason why most people will never get close to a large rocket ready for action is not "security" but their own safety. The large rocket motors of today are capable of burning more than 300 pounds of fuel per second. And anything that swallows that much fuel is obviously very powerful. It is not to be handled casually. If any curious visitors were around, they would only interfere with the work.

Even when visitors are admitted, say at the White Sands Proving Ground in New Mexico, they have to stay half a mile away. It turns out, however, that this is a fine distance for watching. You can really see what is going on. You can see the rocket rising slowly and, moving faster every second, disappear in the sky. If you were permitted to approach more closely, you would have to be in a concrete shelter where there is little to see but dials and instruments. And the view through the periscopes is very limited. So you are really better off seeing it on film where close-ups (through the periscope) and "long shots" from half a mile away can be put together for a complete picture.

When you see such a film on your television screen, you'll be able to observe a few things which are not easy to see when you are actually there. You can see, for example, that there are three successive steps in a V-2 take-off. At first you see just a shower of sparks coming out of the tail end. These sparks are caused by a fireworks pinwheel—electrically ignited—burning inside the rocket motor. This pinwheel is the ignition. As soon as the firing officer sees these sparks falling he knows that the rocket is ready for what is called Preliminary Stage. The valves are opened electrically, the fuels fall into

Foreword

the rocket motor from the fuel tanks, they catch fire and the exhaust flame begins to form. After a second or two the firing officer can tell whether the motor is burning properly. If it is, he orders: "Main Stage On!" This means that the fuel pumps get going and the rocket motor is force-fed, the flame increases in size and in power and reaches its full strength another two seconds later. Then the rocket lifts itself off the firing table to begin the journey beyond the stratosphere.

While the film can show things that are hard to see directly, two things are lacking. One is color—especially on television, but that will be added in time. The other thing that is very nearly lacking is the sound, even though the loudspeaker seems to thunder. No loudspeaker built can even approximately reproduce the sound of a big take-off. A large rocket is not only a magnificent spectacle. It is also—if only accidentally—the loudest noisemaker ever invented. One more thing the film cannot do is to tell just why things are done the way they are done. To discover the reasons, you need books like the one you are reading right now. Maybe it will start you on the way to become a rocket engineer and to contribute your own share to this new science.

Willy Ley

All About Rockets and Jets

1

Fireworks in China

When you are at a beach sometime, watch someone dive from a float. Especially if it is a small one. You will notice that as the diver leaves the float, it is pushed down into the water.

Or get someone to tell you what happened when he fired a gun. As the bullet left one end of the gun, the other end came back to hit him on the shoulder. The force that made the gun kick back and the force that drove the float into the water are the same. It is called *reaction*.

Reaction happens whenever there is action. The diver's jumping and the explosion of the cartridge that held the bullet were actions. When you jump up and down on the ground, there is a reaction in the earth; but you are so small compared to the earth that it does not matter. Reaction is the force that sends a rocket soaring more than a hundred miles into the sky.

A rocket is often called a *reaction engine*. It is the simplest form of engine there is. Nothing in a rocket engine has to turn around or go up and down. It simply starts going and keeps on as long as it has fuel.

You can make a little rocket-engined motorboat for yourself. Cut a piece of wood this shape:

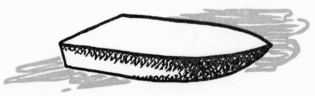

Now get a large capsule from a drug store and glue it to the stern end of your boat, on the bottom side.

When the glue is dry, fill the capsule with Seidlitz powders, the blue and white mixed. (You get them at the same drug store where you got the capsule.) Drop your boat in a bathtub full of water. There will be a reaction between the water and the Seidlitz powder. It turns to a gas. The gas takes up more space than the dry Seidlitz powder did. It cannot get away forward because the capsule holds it in at that end. So it rushes out at the back and as it does so, drives your boat forward. Not very fast or very far, because your engine is a weak one. But it will show what happens.

The biggest rockets ever built work just the same way. Nothing matters except what happens in the firing chamber where the fuel is burned. Your capsule is "the firing chamber" of your little boat. A rocket is a kind of gun wherein we are interested in moving the gun, not the bullet. There isn't any bullet. Instead of it there comes out of the mouth of the rocket a stream of burning gas. This is the result of burning something in the firing chamber.

The Chinese invented rockets many hundred years ago. They were great people to make fireworks, and had firecrackers much before this. Probably one of them noticed the kind of firecracker called a *squizz*. Instead of blowing up the way a firecracker should, a squizz shoots a jet of flame out the fuse end. When this happens the squizz jumps around. This probably gave some Chinese the idea of building a big firecracker that would squizz on purpose.

To do this he left the fuse end of the firecracker open, so that instead of going off with a bang, the powder would burn more slowly. Then he pointed the other end up in the air. The first rockets were probably not very good. A rocket is the simplest engine, but the things that go with it are sometimes difficult. Right at the beginning, the Chinese must have found out that it is hard to make a rocket go in the direction you wish. It is not easy to pack the powder in a rocket so that it will burn evenly. Some grains of powder are larger than others.

When the powder does not burn evenly, the side where it is burning faster has more flame coming out. It pushes the rocket harder and makes it turn in the wrong direction, like this:

There used to be the same trouble about arrows. But long ago people learned that if you put three feathers at the rear end of an arrow, it will not

The Chinese invented rockets hundreds of years ago.

wobble as it flies. When the Chinese tried putting a feathered stick at the end of their rockets to keep them steady, they quickly found that the feathers burned away. So they made the arrow-like sticks on their rockets longer and longer. After a while they found that if they made the stick exactly seven times as long as the rocket, it didn't need any feathers.

The Chinese also invented two other things that are still found in fireworks rockets. One of these was a point or cone on the head of the rocket, so it would fly better than if it had a blunt head. This turned out to be very useful, because they could pack some extra powder into the point and arrange to have it go off with a bang, all at once, when the rocket struck the target.

In fireworks rockets today, this pointed nose is filled with materials that make the colored stars you see when a rocket has gone as high as it can.

The other Chinese invention was the shape of the powder in the rocket. If the rocket is simply stuffed full of powder like a firecracker, it is much more likely to burn unevenly. In addition, there should be as much powder as possible burning at the very minute the rocket is lighted. This gives it a good start. So the Chinese scooped out little holes in the powder. If one of the rockets were cut in two, it would look like this:

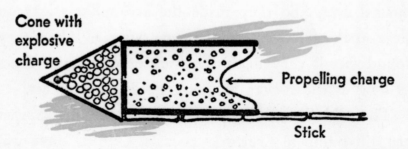

Cone with explosive charge

Propelling charge

Stick

Nowadays there is a better way of giving the right shape to the powder in the rocket than digging some of it out. A long piece of wood called a *thorn* is placed on a bench. Around it is placed the cardboard cylinder that will be the rocket. Around this again is a metal cylinder to hold the cardboard together. A heavy press now squeezes the powder down around the thorn. Then a layer of clay is placed at the lower end, and a cup-shaped hole is bored through it. This hole is the nozzle. It helps to keep the burning gases coming out in a straight line.

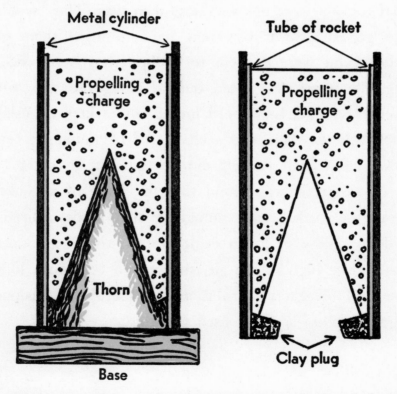

Making rockets is not a job to try at home. It is extremely dangerous even in a scientific laboratory.

All About Rockets and Jets

The Chinese first used rockets at a town named Kai-fung-fu, more than seven hundred years ago. They fired them at the Mongols who were besieging the town, and the Mongols' horses all ran away. But the Mongols came back to take the town later, so the rockets didn't really do much good.

After the siege of Kai-fung-fu, it was quickly found that rockets were not very useful in war. They would not go far, and it was very hard to make them go where you wanted them to. When they were made big, the paper case often burned along the side, and then the rocket blew up. Chinese armies kept on using rockets when there was a chance of frightening a few horses. But their rockets did not amount to much.

However, it was found that the head of a rocket could be loaded with something that made a bright red or yellow or green explosion. As these explosions took place high in the air, they could be seen a long way off. Rockets were therefore useful for making signals. They are still used for this.

2

"The Rockets' Red Glare"

Sometime about 1760, a man whose name we do not even know was working for Raja Hyder Ali in India. His people were not very good with guns and did not have many of them, so he thought he would try rockets. He had the bright idea that if the powder of a rocket could be placed in an iron tube instead of a paper case, you could make as big a rocket as you wished. A big rocket would fly farther.

Soon Hyder Ali had a large number of rockets that would fly more than half a mile. They used twenty-foot poles for sticks. They were not much better at hitting anything they were aimed at than the Chinese rockets. But as Hyder Ali was very rich, he had enough rockets made to be sure of hitting something.

Hyder Ali used his rockets in battles with the English. This caused an Englishman named Sir William Congreve to wonder whether the rocket could not be made into a real weapon, and he began experimenting. He soon found that he could build rockets that would carry more than a mile. They had charges of powder in their heads and would blow up when they hit anything.

Congreve soon found that the bigger he made his rockets, the longer he had to make the sticks. Finally he made the sticks from long pieces of iron. But while the stick was at one side, as it is in a fireworks rocket, these big rockets would not balance properly. It was also very troublesome to carry around these rockets with their long sticks.

So Congreve made two inventions that are important in rocket history. One was to place the stick at the center of the base of the rocket. When this was done, the nozzle could no longer take up the whole base. So instead of one nozzle, Congreve had five. Each one was a little apart from the rest, so the base of the rocket head looked like the picture on page 13.

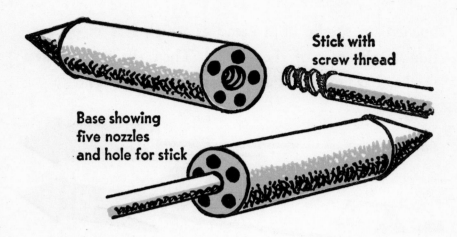

Stick with
screw thread

Base showing
five nozzles
and hole for stick

The stick of Congreve's rocket screwed into the base.

The stick could now be carried separately and screwed into the base of the rocket when it was to be used.

Congreve's rockets were quite a success. The British used them in 1814 to bombard Fort McHenry which guards the city of Baltimore. Francis Scott Key saw the British rockets as he watched the bombardment. Later he wrote of "the rockets' red glare" in "The Star-Spangled Banner" which is now our national anthem.

These rockets may have made a red glare, but they usually failed to hit what they were aimed at. The trouble was that when a rocket started out, it was nicely balanced by the stick. But as it flew, its fuel burned up so the head came to weigh less in proportion to the rest of the rocket. Then the stick pulled the head around and the rocket wobbled in flight.

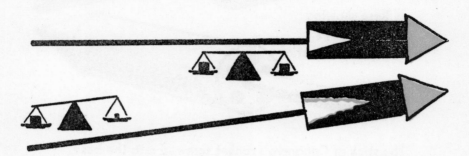

No really useful rockets were made until someone found how to get rid of that stick. For many years different armies tried to make rockets work, but because of the sticks they could not get them to hit their targets.

About the middle of the last century an English engineer named Hale finally thought of a way of making a rocket without a stick. Right at the base of the rocket he placed a ring holding three metal vanes. These were at a small angle.

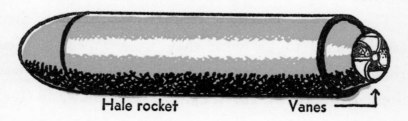

Hale rocket   Vanes

When the burning gas came out of the rocket, it struck these vanes. The whole rocket turned round and round, corkscrewing its way through the air. Bullets turn in the air in the same way. This keeps them flying steadily along the line they start.

But when Hale made this invention, it was too late for rockets to become important. Guns had improved so much that they could shoot farther than any rocket. They were also better at hitting a target. Even more serious was still another defect in Hale's rockets. They were affected by changes in the weather.

This was because they were filled with black powder. Cartridges for guns were also filled with black powder, but it was rather loosely packed. To make a rocket that will go a long distance, the powder has to be squeezed very tight. Now if the weather grows hot or cold, the powder cracks. When it is lighted, the flame does not burn evenly, but runs up the cracks.

The powder is now burning too fast in too many places and the rocket blows up.

The powder will also crack if the rocket is dropped or jarred while being moved around in a train or a truck. This is just as bad. By 1900 every country in the world had decided rockets were not of much use as weapons.

People kept on using them for signals and fireworks.

The Congreve rocket is carrying a rope to the stranded ship.

They were also used in lifesaving. Several people had the idea of tying a small rope to the tail of a Congreve rocket and firing it over a ship stranded on the beach in a storm. A heavier rope is attached to the light one. The people on the ship can then pull in the heavy rope, and get safely ashore in a breeches buoy attached to the rope.

This is one use for rockets in which it doesn't matter if you hit what you aim at, because you don't want to hit anything. These rockets have saved many hundreds of lives, and are still used.

3

New Shapes and Sizes

When chemists discovered explosives that would keep better and burn faster than black powder, people began to think about using rockets as weapons again. They thought about them in different ways in different countries, and what happened in each country is a separate story.

In England they thought of rockets as something to use in shooting down airplanes. Airplanes had begun to fly so fast that they were hard to hit with guns. And it is hard to move a heavy gun around. With rockets, all you have to carry is a light launching tube. Also it is possible to fire a number of rockets at one time. This makes what is called a *barrage*. Many of the rockets will miss, of course, but only one needs to hit.

The first modern war rockets were English. In the beginning they trailed long wires behind them to catch the propellers of the planes. But the British soon found this was not so good as putting explosives in the head of the rockets and firing a barrage.

The Germans thought about rockets as something that would let them shoot a great many shells into a small space at the same time. Their first war rockets were all intended to do this, although they were of different kinds.

The Russians thought of rockets in a different way. An airplane has a hard time fighting a tank, because the bullets from its small guns bounce off the tank's armor, and the plane cannot carry big guns. The Russians thought of a rocket as something that could do the work of a big gun and be carried by a plane to fight tanks.

In the United States, people began thinking of rockets as something that would help an airplane get into the air with a heavy load. Later on, all these countries built all the different kinds of rockets, but each one started out with only one kind.

Wherever they started, they soon found that although a rocket is the simplest engine there is, a good many things about it are far from simple. In the first place, the new explosives burned too fast. The rockets blew up instead of flying. The chemists had to work a long time to find something they could mix with the explosives to make them burn more slowly.

The next problem was that the new explosives gave off a great deal of heat when they burned. This heat would run along the metal case faster than the charge was burning and set fire to the explosive in the nose of the rocket. Then it blew up.

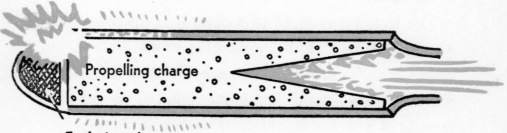

Propelling charge

Explosive charge

The rocket makers solved this by lining the case with something that would not let much heat through. But almost everything they used in the lining swelled when the weather was hot and shrank when it was cold. This left a little space between the lining and the charge. When this happened, the fire would run along the space and once more the rocket blew up.

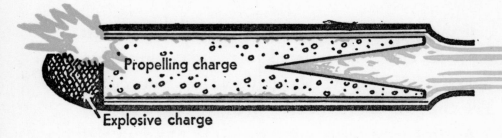

Propelling charge

Explosive charge

It took a long time to overcome these troubles. The British held their experiments in Jamaica, where the temperature does not change much. The Americans did theirs in New Mexico, where it does not change much, either.

While they were at it, they found that the shape of the charge in the old fireworks rockets was not good enough. Rockets with charges shaped in this way turned very fast at the start, but more slowly later. This often made them wobble as they flew. It was one of the main reasons why they failed to hit what they aimed at.

What the rockets needed was a charge that would burn at the same rate all the time. All sorts of shapes were tried. One of the best was the *unrestricted burning charge.*

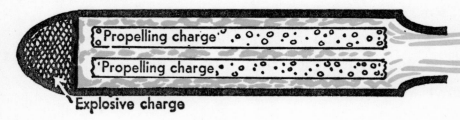

Propelling charge

Propelling charge

Explosive charge

In this the flame starts both on the outside of the charge and in the tube at the center. As the outside burns down and grows smaller, the tube on the inside grows larger. The charge is always burning evenly.

Another good shape was used in the American war rocket called the *Holy Moses*. It would look like this if you could cut it across:

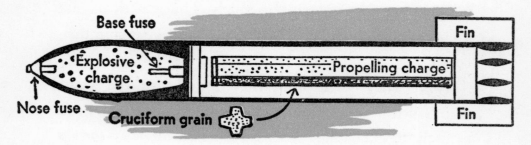

Base fuse
Explosive charge
Nose fuse
Cruciform grain
Propelling charge
Fin
Fin

This is called the *cruciform* shape, and it burns very steadily.

You may ask how they found out exactly what part of a charge burned first. One way is by running rods of something that does not burn at all, or burns very slowly, through the charge. When one of these rods grows very hot, the charge around it must be burning.

Rockets are usually tested by holding a firing chamber down firmly and measuring how strongly the charge is pushing during each small part of a second. The amount of push a rocket gives is called the *thrust*.

Rockets are always spoken of by the amount of thrust they produce. The thrust is measured in pounds. It tells how much weight it would take to hold the rocket down.

Another problem for the rocket makers was how to keep their rockets steady while flying. Keeping them steady is called *stabilization*, and there are two ways of doing it.

One is the way used by an arrow. If it tries to get out of line, the pressure of the air on its feathers brings it back. This is called *fin stabilization*.

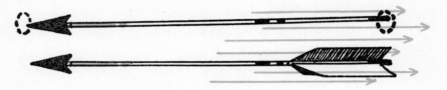

The other way is to set the rocket spinning rapidly, like a bullet or the old Hale rockets. This is called *spin stabilization*.

Neither one is perfect for all rockets. The rocket makers soon found that Hale's way of getting spin stabilization by putting vanes in the blast of the rocket used up a lot of power. This made the rocket fly more slowly than they wished.

But fin stabilization had troubles, too. The fins had

to be folded back against the rocket while it was being launched from its tube. This could be done, with strong springs to bring the fins out as soon as the rocket was in the air. But the time when a rocket most needs stabilization is during the first few tenths of a second it is in the air. If the fins are busy unfolding at this time, they cannot be doing their job of stabilization.

Fuse

Explosive charge

Propelling charge

Fin

Fin

Tube

Bombardment rocket

The fins open as the charge leaves the tube.

Another trouble with fin stabilization is that the rocket needs very large fins at the start of its flight, while the charge is burning. Later on, it only needs small ones. The large fins become so much extra weight, and they may make the rocket steer badly. So everyone began looking for ways to get spin stabilization.

There is one way of doing this that everyone knew about. This was to give the rocket several small nozzles instead of one big one. These nozzles are set at a small angle to the line of the rocket.

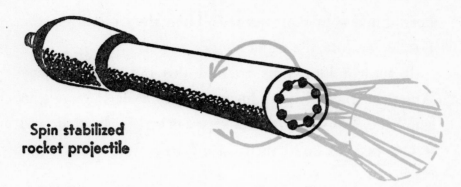

Spin stabilized rocket projectile

The blast coming out of each nozzle now tries to push the rocket off at an angle. But each one is balanced by another nozzle on the opposite side of the rocket, trying to push it in another direction.

This is a good way to get stabilization. But it also caused the rocket to lose some power. And for a long time nobody knew how much a rocket had to spin to remain steady.

The next idea was not to stabilize the rocket at all. Instead, a big tube would be set spinning by a motor, and the rocket fired from it while it was spinning. This worked very well indeed. But when the soldiers saw it, they knew that the tube and its motor were altogether too big and heavy to be carried around.

However, the spinning tube taught the rocket makers one thing. Sometimes it was turned very fast, sometimes more slowly. From it the rocket makers learned just how much spin they needed. Then they could set the nozzles at just the right angle.

It took a long time to find this out. Scarcely any American rockets used during World War II were spin stabilized. Fin stabilized rockets worked fairly well, and it was easy to build them in a hurry.

4

Rockets in World War II

There were more different kinds of rockets used during World War II than you might think.

The Germans were the first to fire rockets from one place on the ground to another. They used three different kinds. Two of them were fired from something called a *Nebelwerfer*. This looked like a very short cannon with six barrels. It fired rockets which were almost six inches in diameter.

One of these Nebelwerfer rockets was built the way you would expect. It had the rocket charge at the rear and the explosive charge in the head, where it would go off when it struck something.

The other was quite different. Instead of having the

rocket behind the explosive charge, it was placed out ahead. The nozzles of this rocket fired in a circle around the explosive charge beneath a kind of metal petticoat.

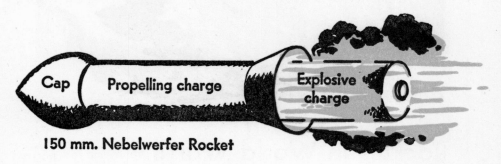

150 mm. Nebelwerfer Rocket

At first the explosive charge had been placed in the cap of the rocket. But in test firings the Germans found that the nose buried itself in the ground before it had time to explode and the soil just stopped the splinters produced by the explosion.

The two Nebelwerfer rockets would fire to a distance of over six miles. They were not very good at hitting things, but this did not matter. The Germans used a great many of them, all at once. When a whole shower of rockets came down in a small space, something was bound to be hit.

One thing prevented the Germans from using more of these rockets. When a Nebelwerfer was fired, the

The Nebelwerfer left long trails of fire across the sky.

rockets left long trails of fire across the sky. It was easy for the enemy to see where they came from. Then the enemy could use their big guns to shoot back, and that was too bad for the Nebelwerfers.

The third kind of German rocket was more than eight inches through. In its nose, or *war head*, it carried a big drum filled with a mixture of oil and gasoline.

The whole thing looked like a huge club. When it struck something, the oil and gasoline would start burning and spread.

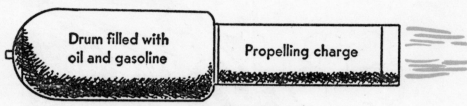

German incendiary rocket

There was one quite new thing about this big fire rocket. It came in a case which was also its launching tube. But it was not very useful. It would only shoot about a mile.

Toward the end of the war, the Germans also began using small rockets fired from one airplane at another.

The Japanese used copies of the German rockets, in addition to a very big one of their own. It had been put together in a great hurry and almost never hit anything.

But the Japanese found quite a new way to use rockets in war. This was in a small airplane, with short, stubby wings. In the tail was a powerful rocket. The nose, or war head, was packed with over a ton of explosives. This airplane had no landing gear, because it was not expected to land. It was carried by a larger

Over a ton of explosives was packed into the war head of the baka, a Japanese rocket plane released by the bomber.

plane to some place near an American fleet. The pilot of the big plane then dropped the rocket plane, and the man in the rocket plane steered it to crash into a ship.

This was called the *baka*. Baka means *fool*, and the pilots of these rocket planes were certainly very foolish. They were all killed, and most of them did not hit the ships they aimed at. It turned out that the baka was too hard to steer, but nobody found out about that during the war because none of the pilots lived to tell about it.

Most of the other rockets used in the war were American or English, or copies of American and English rockets. There were several families of them.

First of all were the *boosters*. These began with the idea of helping an airplane get into the air quickly. Working up enough speed to get off the ground is always the hardest part of a flight. In addition, the United States Navy had a number of aircraft carriers. There is not much room on a carrier's deck to work up speed. So the Navy decided to use rockets to help its planes get away. After the rockets had burned out, the cases could be dropped.

The main trouble was finding the right kind of fuel. These boosters were not intended to fly through the air and hit things, only to give a push. But the fuel had to burn at just the right speed to give this push. The fuels used in the other war rockets burned too fast. Black powder burned too slowly, and besides, it was dangerous.

In addition, the fuel had to be something that would work just as well when it was very hot or very cold as at any other time. That was because American airplanes were used in all kinds of climate all over the world. It took two years to find the right fuel, but now these boosters are a great success. They are called *Jato units,* for *Jet Assisted Take Off.* Now aircraft carriers generally use catapults to shoot planes into the

Jato units are used by heavy bombers.

air, but Jato units are used on big seaplanes and many others.

The next type of rocket made in the United States was a good deal like this. It was a rocket for helping airplane bombs get a good start. Airplanes often have to bomb forts or ships that are protected by armor. If the bomb is dropped from low down, it might not go through the armor. If it is dropped from high up, it might not hit the target. So rockets were built like small Jato units. They were placed in the tails of bombs to make them go faster.

M-8 rockets were used by American forces in World War II.

None of them was used during World War II. Before these rockets were ready, several people began to think that there was not much use placing a weak rocket in the tail of a bomb, when you could make a really strong rocket and shoot it right at the target. The engineers worked out the rocket called the *M-8* which was to be carried by airplanes.

The M-8 was four and a half inches through and weighed thirty-eight pounds. Fin stabilization was quite all right for it, since it was being fired from airplanes going at more than 300 miles an hour. The M-8 was hung under the wings of a plane. When the pilot wished to hit something, he pointed his plane at it and fired the rockets.

The M-8 was a very useful rocket. Airplanes fired them at bridges, forts, trains, tanks, groups of trucks or anything else that could not be reached by guns on the ground. The Russians used M-8 rockets and some of their own which were copied from the M-8. The Germans called them *Black Death*. They hit the tops of the German tanks, where the armor was thinnest, and often burst inside.

Toward the end of the war the American Air Force began using the rocket they called the *Holy Moses*. It was almost twice as heavy and powerful as the M-8. Very few things could stand up against the Holy Moses.

But there was one thing that could. On some of the Pacific islands the Japanese would hollow out the whole inside of a mountain. Tunnels led to the outside, where there were armored doors with guns behind them.

The Holy Moses could not crack this. So a very big American rocket was built, called *Tiny Tim*. It was over ten feet long and more than eleven inches through the middle. An airplane could not carry many Tiny Tims, but when one hit something, it hit hard.

These were all rockets to be carried by airplanes. There were also rockets to be fired from the ground or from ships. They began with the M-8. The American Army quickly found that the M-8 was not very good at hitting any one thing. But when M-8s were used in a barrage, like the German rockets, they covered a whole area at once. The Army built a launching rack called the *Calliope*, from which sixty rockets could be fired at almost the same time.

The Calliope, a 60-tube launching rack, is mounted on a tank.

These rockets could only travel a little over two miles. This is less than most guns shoot. If the Calliope were placed in position and the rockets fired, the enemy could see where the rockets came from and shoot back with guns. So the Calliope was usually placed on a jeep or on top of a tank. When it had fired once, it would go somewhere else. Once was usually enough when the target was reasonably small.

But there were times when the Navy wanted to hit quite large targets very fast. This was when the Navy had to land troops on a shore held by the enemy. Soldiers in boats going ashore cannot fight back. Some way had to be found to keep the enemy from shooting at them. The best way would be to shoot at the enemy so fast he could not fire at the soldiers trying to land.

The Navy worked with the Army on the M-8 for this. The Navy had one advantage. When rockets were fired from the ground, they had to be fired from tubes. This meant they were stabilized with folding fins; and as we have seen, this is not a very good way. But on a ship there is plenty of room. The rockets could be fired from open racks, so their fins did not have to fold back.

The space on a ship also helped in another way. On

land it is hard to get as many rocket projectors as you wish into one place. But on a ship you can set up as many as the deck will hold, all in one place. A number of landing craft were rebuilt into rocket ships, called *LSM (R)*. They were used for the first time in the invasion of Sicily in 1943.

The LSM (R) releasing a barrage of M-8 rockets in World War II.

They did not look very pretty, but each rocket ship could fire 1,020 rockets in a minute. This is two and a half times as much fire as the largest battleship can put out. When such numbers of rockets began to come down, everything around where they hit was torn to pieces. Mines blew up, barbed wire was broken, machine guns were knocked out, and men in heavy forts were stunned by the explosions.

After this, rocket ships were used whenever landings were made. Toward the end of the war a spin-stabilized rocket five inches through was worked out, and this was even better.

5

Seagoing Rockets

All these rockets were used against targets on the ground. In addition, several kinds of rockets were built for use against Japanese and German submarines.

One was intended for airplanes to fire at a submarine when they found it on the surface. This was a strange rocket, smaller than the M-8, but much heavier. There was no explosive charge. Much of the weight was in a solid steel head. When you hit a submarine with something, it is not necessary to have an explosion. If you make a hole in the submarine, the water will do the rest. This rocket had a very heavy charge to give it great speed and drive it right through the submarine.

The second anti-submarine rocket was like those used

The bomb is carried far ahead by the speed of the plane.

to boost bombs, but it worked in the opposite direction. A submarine under water can often be seen from an airplane. But if the airplane drops a bomb at once, it will miss. The bomb will be carried far ahead by the speed of the plane.

So when a submarine is located, the plane has to circle and come back. Even then the airplane pilot has a hard time. He has to guess where the submarine is before he drops his bomb. And the submarine may have moved while he was circling.

To get over this difficulty, the Navy invented the *retro-rocket*. When it was attached to a bomb, the pilot dropped the bomb right over the submarine. The

The retro-rocket drops straight down on the submarine.

rocket fired backward to get rid of the speed of the plane, and the bomb dropped straight down. The last German submarine sunk during the war was sent down by a retro-rocket bomb.

The third kind of anti-submarine rocket was not carried by airplanes, but by ships. It was fired from something called a *hedgehog*. Before the hedgehog was invented, the only way of damaging a submarine under water was with depth charges. These are huge cans of explosives, set to go off at a certain depth under water. They are intended to blow in a submarine's side.

The only way to find out where a submarine is hidden under water is to listen for the sound its propeller makes. Instruments magnify this sound and show what direction it is coming from. But when two or three depth charges go off under water, the sound is so loud that the men at the instruments are deafened, and the instruments themselves are sometimes broken. If the submarine is not hit the first time, it may get away.

The hedgehog rocket projector holds twenty-four rockets.

The hedgehog was invented to overcome this trouble. It is a kind of box in the bow of a ship and holds twenty-four rockets.

All are fired at the same time. They fly into the air and arch over into the water in a "spread," a small distance from each other.

Hedgehog rockets are much smaller than depth charges, but they will not go off until they hit something. When the men aboard a ship hear a hedgehog explosion, they know they have hit the submarine, and they also know exactly where it is. Since the explosion is a small one, no one aboard the ship is deafened.

More submarines were sunk by rockets and retro-bombs and hedgehogs than by anything else.

Under hedgehog attack, many rockets can be sent smashing down on the enemy submarine.

6

The Bazooka and Mickey Mouse

Of all the American rockets used during the war, the most famous was the *bazooka*.

This weapon was built for use against tanks and concrete forts. A tank has so much armor that an ordinary bullet will not go through it. For use against tanks, some countries built big, heavy rifles that needed two operators. But these rifles were not much better. Most countries tried to stop tanks with small cannon, but it took several men to handle one of these guns. When cannons came into use, the makers of the tanks simply put on more armor.

The bazooka depends upon something called the *Munroe effect*. When a ball or cylinder of explosive goes off, the force of the explosion spreads in all directions from the center.

But if the explosive is cup-shaped, something strange happens inside the cup. The force of the explosion from all around the edges of the cup goes toward the center. There it meets the force coming from all the other sides of the cup, as well as the force from the bottom. Since there is more explosive at the bottom of the cup, the whole explosion is driven toward the mouth. At the same time, all this force is added up and becomes much more powerful.

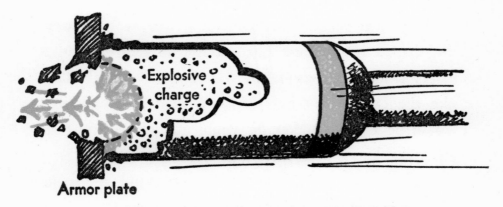

Armor plate

A shaped charge can blow holes in steel armor plate.

This is the Munroe effect, and anything that uses it is called a *shaped charge*. It was known for a long time that a shaped charge would blow holes in a steel plate that would keep out bullets or shells. But this was only part of the story. If the shaped charge is going to blow a hole in a steel plate, it has to go off a tiny bit in front of the plate to give the parts of the explosion a chance to get together. So the shaped charge has to have a cap.

Now if a shaped charge is put in a shell and fired from a gun, the cap crumples up when it strikes the target. The shaped charge itself crumples up before it can go off, and the parts of the explosion cannot get together to make a hole in the plate. That is, a gun drives the charge too *fast* for it to be useful.

What was needed was something that would carry the shaped charge just fast enough so that it would barely reach the plate before the charge went off. The idea the U.S. Army men had was that this something would be a small rocket. It would not have to start at top speed like a shell from a gun.

It took quite a while to find the right kind of charge for the rocket. It had to be one that would burn all its fuel in the launching tube, or the man using it would get some of the blast in his face. In the end, the bazooka was a long folding tube which one man held on his shoulder while another fired the rocket.

When it was finished, the Army had a weapon with which two men, using a rocket weighing only a few pounds, could blow a hole in the side of a heavily-armored tank. Nothing went into the tank but the explosion, but that was enough. It burned out everything inside.

The bazooka was very important in winning the war. When the enemy made tanks with more armor, the answer was to make a bigger bazooka.

Since the end of the war, many new kinds of rockets have been made all over the world. Most of them

A bazooka could blow a hole in a heavily armored tank.

are kept secret. One of the most interesting is the *Mickey Mouse*. This is quite a small rocket, only a few inches through. The Mickey Mouse is used by one airplane to fire at another. It is something like a bazooka and something like a hedgehog. It is like a hedgehog because several are fired at one time, and they spread out as they fly. It is like a bazooka because the head holds a shaped charge.

7

Liquid-Fuel Rockets

All the rockets mentioned so far have been solid-fuel rockets. No matter what they were used for or how they were built, they were really not so very different from the old fireworks rockets.

But there is another family of rockets that has become even more important. These are the liquid-fuel rockets. They started out in quite a different way from the others. All the solid-fuel rockets began as war rockets. When people began building liquid-fuel rockets, they were not thinking of using them in war at all. They were thinking of going to the moon.

When anything rises from the earth, whether it is a stone you throw upward, or a rocket, or a shell from a gun, the earth keeps pulling the object back by the force called *gravity*.

Beyond the thin layer of air right around the earth, there is no air to hold up an airplane or a balloon. No cannon big enough to shoot a shell to the moon can be built. So when people began to think seriously about going to the moon, they knew they would have to use a rocket. But the scientists quickly found that no solid-fuel rocket could make the trip.

The charge in solid-fuel rockets is made up only of the fuel. These rockets take some oxygen from the air in order to burn. Indeed, burning is the business of combining something with oxygen. When oxygen is combined with something else, energy is given off.

Out in space where there is no air, there is no oxygen either. To go to the moon, a rocket must carry its own oxygen. It would be very hard to build a rocket that squirted oxygen into solid fuel and the storage tank for a solid fuel would be so heavy that it would not work well. But there is another and still better reason why a solid-fuel rocket with oxygen would not do.

When anything is burned in a rocket firing chamber, the burning gases rush out the rear end. The speed with which they come out is called *jet velocity* or *exhaust velocity*.

The speed of a rocket depends on the exhaust velocity.

The speed of a rocket depends on its exhaust velocity. The exhaust velocity depends on how fast the fuel burns.

Earlier we saw how much trouble the makers of solid-fuel rockets had in trying to get a fuel that burned slowly enough. If they used something like TNT, which burns very fast, the rocket would blow up.

It is easy to figure out how much exhaust velocity a rocket will have. When this was done with solid-fuel rockets, it was found that none of them had enough exhaust velocity, that is, enough speed to get away from the pull of the earth's gravity. No matter how big they were made, they would have the same exhaust velocity. They would come back to earth.

The rocket makers wanted a fuel that would burn much faster than any solid fuel. But they needed one that could be fed into the firing chamber a little at a time so the rocket would not blow up. They could easily calculate that the only things that would do this were liquids.

So the rocket makers decided on liquids. But they quickly found they had a lot of problems. Even if the rocket never left earth, fuel would have to be sprayed into the firing chamber at one end, while a red-hot jet was coming out the other. There would be no way for oxygen to reach the fuel and make it burn unless it were sprayed in at the same time as the fuel.

Oxygen is a gas. If it stayed that way, not enough oxygen could be brought into the firing chamber to burn the fuel. It takes three and a half pounds of oxygen to burn one pound of gasoline. So the oxygen had to be turned into a liquid by cooling it and pressing it very hard.

But liquid oxygen is not very comfortable stuff to handle. Its temperature is nearly 200 degrees below zero, which means it will seriously hurt anyone it touches. It is always trying to get rid of the pressure holding it in. This means it is apt to blow up the container holding it.

All the same, the rocket makers decided they could not get along without liquid oxygen. Some of them were Germans and some were Americans, but they worked pretty much the same way.

The first question was what fuel to burn with the oxygen. Some people thought one thing would be better, and some thought another, but in the beginning everyone tried gasoline. They knew this would not give enough exhaust velocity to go to the moon. But nobody thought about building a moon rocket right away. They thought they had better learn something about liquid-fuel rockets first. Nobody had ever built a liquid-fuel rocket.

Then came the problem of how to keep the fuel and the liquid oxygen flowing into the firing chamber. Most of the early rocket makers did this by putting some gas under heavy pressure into the tanks full of liquid oxygen to squeeze it into the firing chamber.

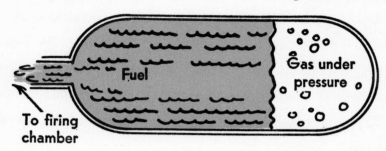

The next question was the shape of the rocket. Everyone agreed that it would be very hard to stabilize a rocket that flew so much faster than any solid-fuel rocket. Also much of the rocket would be made up of fuel tanks. Since there would be no way of bracing the tanks, they would be quite weak.

Both the Germans and the Americans thought of the idea of placing the firing chamber in the very nose of the rocket. Pulling the rest of the rocket along, it would not need to be stabilized so long as it went straight up. And as long as the fuel tanks were being pulled into the air pressing against them, and not pushed, it would not matter if they were weak. All the first liquid-fuel rockets were placed in the nose of the rocket and thus had *nose drive*.

Then came the question of the firing chamber itself.

A solid-fuel rocket burns for only a few seconds. But the men who made the first liquid-fuel rockets wanted something that would burn for a long time, as much as several minutes. And inside the firing chamber of a liquid-fuel rocket it was much hotter than in a solid-fuel rocket. When the makers fired their rockets for four or five seconds, the steel walls of their firing chambers burned through.

This usually made the rockets blow up. The inventors tried making the firing chambers of aluminum, then of porcelain, then of other metals. The porcelain cracked and the metals burned through. It was very perplexing.

The rocket makers decided that the only way to keep the firing chambers from burning through was to cool them with something on the outside. After this, most of the early liquid-fuel rockets had jackets full of water around the firing chamber.

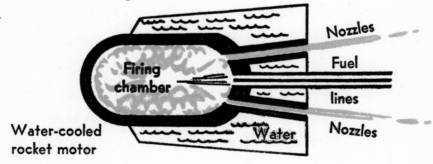

Water-cooled rocket motor

It took years to work these things out. Most of the early liquid-fuel rockets never flew at all. They were mounted on test stands to see how they worked. A few were fired, and one or two of them went a mile up. When you realize that solid-fuel rockets had already gone higher than this, you will understand that not much progress was being made. Then something happened.

The Germans began to think about liquid-fuel rockets as weapons.

When this happened, everything they knew about rockets was kept secret. It stayed secret for eleven years. But before this happened, several people tried to show some of the things rockets might do in the future.

One of these people was named Max Valier. He was an engineer who became interested in building automobiles and airplanes driven by rockets.

A rocket automobile is not a very good idea. The reason is that a rocket does not begin to work very well until it is going at nearly the speed of its exhaust velocity. Unless it is going this fast the rocket is not efficient. That is, it is too difficult and too expensive to use. It is easier and cheaper to use some other kind of engine. For most rockets the exhaust velocity is several hundred miles an hour. If an automobile went this fast, its tires would burn up.

But Max Valier wanted to get people interested in rockets. He built a car with several powder rockets at the back. As each one would fire only a short time, he set them to fire one after the other. Max Valier's first car was a success, but after this none of them worked right. Usually one or more of the rockets blew up. On his last car, all the rockets blew up together and the car was torn to pieces.

Max Valier was not discouraged. But he had learned that he needed a rocket that would burn for several minutes. So he built a liquid-fuel rocket to drive a car. But it blew up and Max Valier was killed.

About the same time a man named Friedrich Schmiedl in Austria thought of using rockets to carry

mail. Austria has a great many mountains. It may take two whole days to walk around mountains between towns which are really only a few miles apart. Schmiedl thought of shooting the mail over the mountains in rockets.

He used solid-fuel rockets. When the rocket was about to strike the ground, a small charge shot the mail bag out with a parachute and it drifted to earth. This worked quite well, and mail was delivered this way several times. Then the Austrian government made Schmiedl stop. No one knows why.

German Experiments

When the German army began to work on liquid-fuel rockets for war, they thought of them as useful for carrying big charges of explosive over long distances. Airplanes can do this, but there is always a chance that the enemy will shoot an airplane down. A rocket goes too fast to be shot down. A solid-fuel rocket will only go a short distance, five or six miles. The Germans wanted something that would go two or three hundred miles.

There were a lot of problems still to solve. The Germans quickly found that nose-drive rockets would not do. The rocket followed the firing chamber in the nose all right, but when the nose was out of line the tiniest part of an inch, the whole rocket was out of line, too. People who wanted to go to the moon did not mind too much about this. But if a war rocket is going to hit its target, there must be some way of making it fly exactly right.

Also there ought to be some way of changing its direction after it has started. There is a good way of doing this by sending a radio message to the rocket. When the rocket gets the message, an electric circuit is closed and a much stronger current turns part of the mechanism. This is called a *servo-mechanism*.

But if a servo-mechanism is to work, it must have something to work on. Fins outside the rocket, like the tail of an airplane, were the first thing the Germans thought of. But they soon found out that fins outside the rocket were not enough. It took a great deal of power to turn them against the pressure of the air, and by the time they turned, it was too late.

So they went back to vanes in the exhaust just as Hale had done. But the new vanes—there were four of them—were made of graphite and they were movable. When the servo-mechanism moved one of these vanes, it changed the direction of a part of the exhaust blast. The Germans called these vanes "blast rudders."

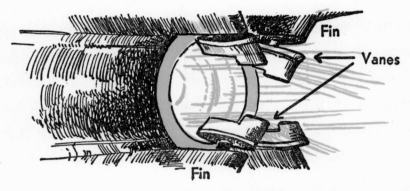

The rocket changed its direction a little as the vanes
pressed against the jet.

Solving one problem in these rockets kept bringing
others up. One of the problems was that after radio
and servo-mechanisms were built in, it had to be a
very large rocket, larger than any built before. This
made new problems. Another problem was that of
cooling the firing chamber, the same problem that
always bothers makers of liquid-fuel rockets.

This was hooked up with the question of what fuel
should be used. Some of the rocket makers had thought
of alcohol in the beginning, but no one had tried it.
Now the Germans found that if they used alcohol as
a fuel, they would have a clever way of keeping the
firing chamber cool enough to prevent its burning
through.

First of all, the alcohol tank was placed so that the

alcohol would come to the firing chamber in a long
tube, running through the tank of liquid oxygen. As
liquid oxygen is so very cold, this made the alcohol
cold when it reached the firing chamber. When the
alcohol arrived, it was sprayed into a burner cup that
would look like this if you cut it in half:

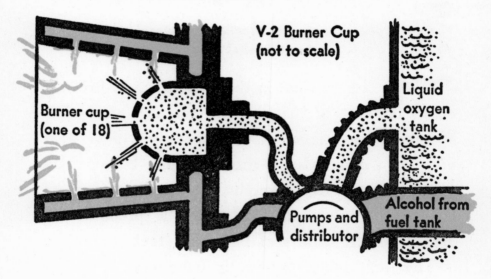

V-2 Burner Cup
(not to scale)

Burner cup
(one of 18)

Liquid
oxygen
tank

Pumps and
distributor

Alcohol from
fuel tank

The oxygen comes in from above. For just a tiny
part of a second the cold alcohol runs along the walls
of the burner cup. It cannot catch fire until it reaches
the oxygen in the middle of the cup. The alcohol stays
long enough to keep the walls from burning through.
This is called *film cooling*.

When the Germans built their big rockets, they had

eighteen of these burner cups arranged around the walls of the firing chamber. By using many small cups, it was easier to keep each one cool.

Another curious thing they found out was that they had to be very careful about the shape of the nozzle of the firing chamber. If it is this shape,

Rocket motor

the exhaust velocity goes up while it is moving at ordinary speeds. But as soon as it reaches the speed at which sound travels through the air, which is 740 miles an hour, this shape makes the exhaust velocity go down instead of up. At a speed of more than 740 miles an hour, the shape of the nozzle has to be like this to make the exhaust velocity go up.

Rocket motor

As the Germans wanted very high speeds, they took the second shape.

Another problem was how to get the fuel and oxygen into the firing chamber. They could not be allowed just to run in because they would not get there fast enough. Also both the fuel and oxygen had to be pushed hard into the firing chamber. The burning going on there makes a great deal of pressure, and this tries to keep new things from coming in.

The rocket engineers had to work out a pump to bring fuel to the firing chamber. This could not be any ordinary pump. It would have to work faster and harder than any pump had worked before.

Finally they invented a new kind of pump. It is run by something called *hydrogen peroxide*. Hydrogen peroxide is made up of two atoms of hydrogen and two atoms of oxygen. H stands for hydrogen and O stands for oxygen. In hydrogen peroxide the atoms are hooked together like this:

$$H\text{-}O\text{-}O\text{-}H$$

Ordinary water is made of two atoms of hydrogen and one of oxygen, hooked up like this:

$$H\text{-}O\text{-}H$$

Hydrogen peroxide does not like to stay together. It has a tendency to give up one of its oxygen atoms and to become water. It is very easy to make hydrogen peroxide do this. When it happens, the mixture of water and left-over oxygen becomes so hot that the water turns to steam.

There will be more about this later, but what you need to know now is that the steam from hydrogen peroxide was used by the Germans to drive the pump for their big rocket. When they had it built, it was the biggest rocket on earth. It was called A-4 or V-2, and looked like this inside.

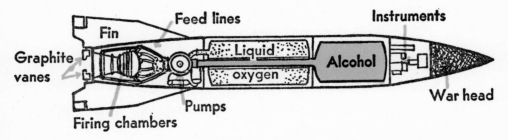

The A-4 or V-2 was nearly 48 feet tall when it stood up on its tail ready to be fired, and it weighed over twelve tons. Its nose, or war head, held nearly a ton of explosives.

But even after the Germans worked out their troubles with cooling the firing chamber and getting the right kind of pumps, they kept having trouble with the big rockets. Only two of the first nineteen worked right. The rest went up a little way and then exploded.

The trouble was that these accidents always happened when the rocket was in the air, going several hundred miles an hour, and nobody could tell what was wrong. The rocket makers finally decided that the rocket moved so fast that the pressure of the air broke in its sides. Then they began putting an iron ring around the outside. After this, the rockets worked better.

The V-2 went nearly 62 miles up, where there is scarcely any air at all. It could be fired to a distance of almost 200 miles. When it was moving as fast as it could, it was going 3,466 miles an hour.

The Germans fired V-2s from Holland across the English Channel at the city of London. It took more than five minutes for the rockets to get there. When they struck, they made terrible explosions, and everything near by was blown to pieces. But less than half the rockets the Germans fired reached London. When you remember that London is a very large city, this record does not look very good, and it was not.

The trouble with the V-2 was that the Germans finished it in too much of a hurry. They had no really good way of making it go where they wanted it to go. When a rocket is moving at over 3,000 miles an hour, a radio signal directing it to change its course will probably get there too late.

The Germans also made several other kinds of liquid-fuel war rockets, but none of them was ready in time to be used in the war. Most of them were intended to be fired at airplanes. One of the most interesting was the *Wasserfall*, which means *waterfall*. It was quite a big rocket, twenty-five and a half feet long.

The German Wasserfall was a liquid-fuel rocket.

The interesting thing about the Wasserfall was that it was the first important liquid-fuel rocket not to use oxygen. Liquid oxygen becomes a gas, or evaporates, very easily. For this reason the Germans always carried their V-2 rockets empty to the place where they were going to be fired. Behind the rocket would come a tank of oxygen. At the last minute before firing, the oxygen would be put in the rocket.

All About Rockets and Jets

Of course some of the oxygen evaporated while it was being poured. This was all right for a big rocket like the V-2. It held over 10,000 pounds of oxygen, and the loss of two or three hundred pounds was not too important. But the Germans could not afford to lose two or three hundred pounds of oxygen in pouring it into a rocket that only carried 1,000 pounds.

There was also another reason for not using oxygen. If you are going to have a rocket to shoot at airplanes, it has to be ready when you hear the airplane coming. There is no time to fill it up with oxygen.

So while the British were making solid-fuel rockets to shoot at airplanes, the Germans were trying to find a good liquid fuel to use in a rocket. This fuel had to be something that did not need pure oxygen to make it burn. It also had to be something that was easy and cheap to make. It had to give off a great deal of energy when it burned. And it had to be something that could be carried around without going off by itself.

On top of that the Germans had to find something to burn the fuel with. After many experiments they chose a fuel called *visol* and used nitric acid to burn it with. This had one great advantage. When nitric acid and visol are mixed, the mixture catches fire by itself. This was what they used in the Wasserfall rocket. To start it going, they only had to open the valves that let the nitric acid and visol flow into the firing chamber.

The Wasserfall had short, stubby wings on its sides to make it fly better. It also had a radio in its nose and fins at the tail. Just behind the nose was a bottle holding compressed air. When the rocket got the right kind of radio message, some of this air would work a servo-mechanism which would change the position of the fins. This steered the rocket.

The idea was that when an enemy airplane appeared overhead, the Wasserfall would be started for it. A radio man on the ground would steer the rocket. When it got close enough to the plane, he would send another kind of message, and the whole rocket would blow up.

But even the Germans thought the Wasserfall was not very practical. It could be carried around with its fuel inside, which the V-2 could not. But it weighed more than four tons and was very expensive. Also Wasserfall rockets did not always work well. Like the V-2 it had been finished too soon.

While the Germans were working on the Wasserfall, they were also building another liquid-fuel rocket called a *Taifun*. The Taifun was quite small, not much bigger than the M-8 rockets used by the American Army and Navy. As they were small and rather cheap, a large number could be built quickly. Also a large number could be fired at once. The Germans expected to use Taifun rockets against airplanes in the same way the U.S. Navy used M-8 rockets against beaches.

The Taifun was a very interesting rocket. It was not big enough to carry all the parts a V-2 or even a Wasserfall had, so the Germans had to find new ways of doing things. This is what it looked like inside:

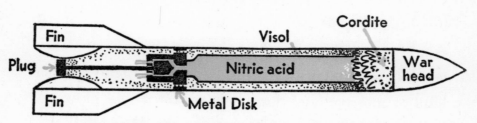

The Taifun was a small liquid-fuel German rocket.

In this picture the tank carrying nitric acid is inside the tank carrying the visol fuel. Toward the nose of the rocket you will see a small patch marked *cordite*, which is an explosive. When the Germans wished to start the rocket, this explosive was set off.

The explosion squeezed down into the fuel and the

nitric acid. At the bottom of the fuel tank there was another little piece of metal. The pressure from above caused this to break, and the fuel ran into the firing chamber. At the very bottom, the nozzle, there was another plug. You can see that a rod from this holds the nitric acid tank shut. The fuel pulled this out. Then the nitric acid joined the visol, there was an explosion, and away went the Taifun.

The Taifun was much faster in getting started than either the V-2 or Wasserfall. It would go all the way up to 50,000 feet, much higher than any airplane can fly. But before the Germans got it working properly, the war was over.

Still another rocket, and one that was used in the war by the Germans, was called *HS-293*. This was a big rocket, quite a lot like the Japanese baka, only it did not have a pilot. It was sometimes called the *glider bomb* or *air torpedo*. It had wings and a rocket in its tail.

The glider bomb was carried by an airplane. It was used against ships. When the pilot of the plane saw an Allied ship, he pulled a lever that let loose the glider bomb, and at the same time started its rocket. The pilot steered the bomb toward the ship by radio signals.

The German glider bomb is in line of fire from 40 mm. guns.

These glider bombs sank several ships. One of them was an Italian battleship. But after a while, the Allies found out that if somebody on the ship set something going that made small electric sparks, the airplane pilot could not control his bomb. The bomb would not come close to anything making an electric spark, which makes a signal like a radio signal. Even the small spark of an electric shaver was enough to send glider bombs rushing off in any direction except the one they were supposed to take.

After this the Germans stopped using glider bombs.

The Germans also made an interesting long-range solid-fuel rocket, called *Rheinbote*, or "Messenger from the Rhine." This was over 37 feet long and made of three parts.

It had a booster, or explosive charge, to help it start. When the bottom end of the rocket had finished burning, it dropped away, and then the second section fired. This also dropped away after it was empty, and the long slender rocket with its war head went on. This kind of rocket is known as a step rocket. It is quite useful because the last step does not have to carry the weight of the steps that went before and can make more speed.

The Rheinbote, over 37 feet long, could travel 137 miles.

The Rheinbote was fired from a big steel girder, and was aimed like a gun. It could go 137 miles, which is very good indeed for a solid-fuel rocket. No other rocket using solid fuel ever did that well. The Germans fired a number of Rheinbote rockets, mostly at the city of Antwerp.

But the Rheinbote was, after all, not a very good rocket except at setting records for distance. When it took off, it weighed 3,773 pounds. So much of this weight was taken up by fuel and the cases to hold it that the war head had only 88 pounds of explosive. This is less than a large shell. And when you add the fact that it is just about impossible to hit anything smaller than a large city from 137 miles away, you can see why the Rheinbote never amounted to much.

9

Uncle Sam's Rockets

Since the war many other types of rockets have been built, but the government does not like to talk about them very much. Nearly all fighter planes now use rockets instead of guns. Two of the most interesting big rockets are the Army Nike and the Air Force Matador.

The Nike is a slender anti-aircraft rocket. At its base it has another rocket, a booster to get it very quickly into the air. This booster uses solid fuel and drops away as soon as the liquid fuel in the Nike begins firing.

The Nike is more than just a rocket. It can be guided to its target by radio. When it gets close to the enemy airplane, it sends out radar waves and catches them as they bounce back.

Then it follows the target. No amount of dodging by a plane can keep it away from a Nike.

The Matador is a missile that can carry an atom bomb. It has a booster like the Nike, and can be guided by radio signals. When the Matador starts, these signals are from the ground. But the Matador can travel more than 200 miles, and people on the ground could not follow it that far. So the Matador can also be guided from a plane in the air. Since it flies much faster than any plane, the plane has to be already in the air, somewhere near the target. The pilot of the plane is notified

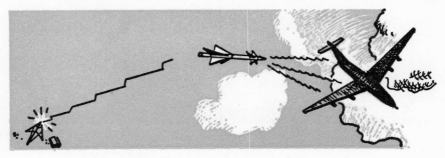

The Nike is guided to its target by radar.

by radio that a Matador is coming. Then he guides it to the target.

The Nike and Matador are called *guided missiles*. There are several other kinds of guided missiles. The Navy has one called the *Terrier*, which rides to its target along a radio beam.

War rockets are not the only kind now being used. As soon as military men began firing rockets high up in the air, scientists realized what a wonderful opportunity this was. They knew very little about the air far above them. How cold or hot was it at different heights? Was the air at these heights made up in a

At first the Matador travels on ground signals. Then it is guided to the target by a plane already in the air.

different way from the air close to the earth? And what kind of rays from the sun or stars were roaming around up there? Rockets could take up instruments and answer these questions.

So two very interesting rockets were built to search the upper air. They were called the *Aerobee* and the *Viking*. The Aerobee is a little over 18 feet long and 15 inches through. It is a liquid-fuel rocket with a

Cameras in the Aerobee can take pictures from 50 miles up.

solid-fuel booster. It carries instruments in its nose, and these instruments radio back to the ground what they find. Sometimes the Aerobee takes up cameras, and photographs the earth from over 50 miles up, where no one has ever been.

The Aerobee has no controls except one for cutting off the fuel in case anything goes wrong. But it does not need them because it is not supposed to go anywhere except straight up. Aerobees have flown up to more than 70 miles above the earth.

The Viking is a big rocket, as long as a V-2, but much thinner. It is a lot like a V-2, and was built after American engineers had a chance to look at the V-2 and build a better one. It weighs five tons.

Rocket motor in swivel rings

When the Viking rocket is to change direction, the whole firing chamber turns. The jet goes out at a different angle.

One of the interesting things about the Viking is the way it is controlled. The four graphite vanes sticking into the exhaust of the V-2 rocket worked well enough, but they took away some of the power. Now their purpose was to deflect a part of the exhaust jet. Why not deflect the whole exhaust jet?

The designers of the Viking rocket mounted the whole rocket motor into swivel rings. (These swivel rings are called gimbals.) When the rocket tried to tilt, the servo-mechanisms tilted the rocket motor to prevent it.

The high altitude record for the V-2 rocket had been 116 miles. Then a lightened V-2 went to 128 miles. That was its final record. Viking No. VII went to 136 miles in August, 1951. Three years later, in May, 1954, Viking No. XI went to 158 miles.

There is not too much difference between a rocket like the Viking which is built for scientific research and a rocket like the V-2 which was built for military purposes. In fact the V-2 did both. The difference lies first in what is carried. If there is a war head in the nose of the rocket, it is a military rocket. If there is a "package" of scientific instruments, it is a research rocket.

A second difference between a research rocket and a military rocket is the way it is made to fly. A research rocket is supposed to tell us what is going on high in the atmosphere. For this reason you want it to go as high as possible. This means that you fire it vertically into the air, or very nearly so. The vertical shot has another result too. It will make the rocket fall back fairly near the place from which it was fired. If this place is a large proving ground, this makes the experiment safer; for there is nobody on a proving ground except those who have some business there. And everybody on a proving ground knows when a large rocket is to be fired.

But a military rocket is supposed to hit a target. So you don't fire it vertically. However, the take-off of the rocket may be vertical. The reason for this is that a large rocket moves quite slowly at first. If you tried to fire it at an angle, it might fall over. When fired vertically, it is more stable. Large military rockets take off vertically for this reason. When they have gathered some speed, a mechanism inside begins to work and tilts them in the direction in which they are supposed to go.

The first of Uncle Sam's military rockets after World War II was one called the Redstone. The name is taken from Redstone Arsenal near Huntsville, Alabama, where the rocket was developed. It can travel about 200 miles like the V-2, but it can carry a war head that weighs several times as much as that of the V-2.

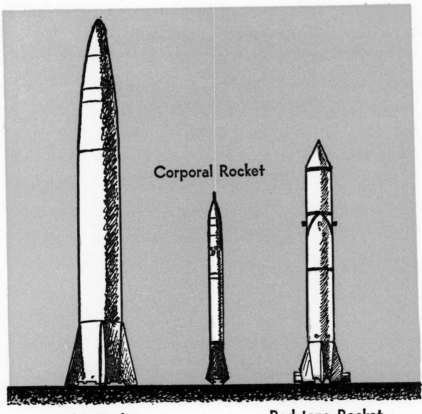

Corporal Rocket

Atlas Rocket

Redstone Rocket

The fuels used in the Redstone rocket are the same that were used in the V-2 and in the Viking, namely alcohol burned with liquid oxygen.

The next military rocket to be built was the Corporal missile. It stands about 45 feet tall, very nearly the same as the V-2 and the Viking, but it uses other fuels. The Corporal's fuels are aniline and nitric acid. It can go as far as 50 miles and is said to be very accurate.

Another new military rocket is the Atlas, which is designed to cross the Atlantic Ocean in one long jump. The Atlas rocket stands over 70 feet tall and has two enormous boosters to assist it when it takes off. The rocket takes off with both boosters burning. The main rocket motor of the Atlas starts up immediately after take-off. The boosters keep burning until they have used up their fuel. Then they drop off. The main motor of the Atlas keeps going until the rocket has the speed it needs to cross the ocean.

The Atlas is a liquid-fuel rocket of such power that its builders have said that it could go all the way to the moon. If an Atlas rocket were fired to the moon, it could not carry its normal heavy war head.

Honest John Rocket

American engineers have also built several large rockets with solid fuels. So much work has been put in on solid fuels in the last ten years that these fuels are safe now. They also can be made into rocket charges of very large size.

The solid-fuel charge that drives the Honest John weighs 2,000 pounds. The war head the rocket carries weighs 1,500 pounds. The Honest John is not, strictly speaking, a missile. It has no guidance. It carries no complicated servo-mechanisms or instruments of any kind. It is just a very large rocket that is fired from a launcher. And the launcher is aimed just like a gun. But Honest John can hit a target 90,000 feet away. At that distance it needs precisely 87 seconds to get from its launcher to the target.

Another larger solid-fuel rocket, built for the U. S. Air Force, is called the X-17. It is also known as a "re-entry missile."

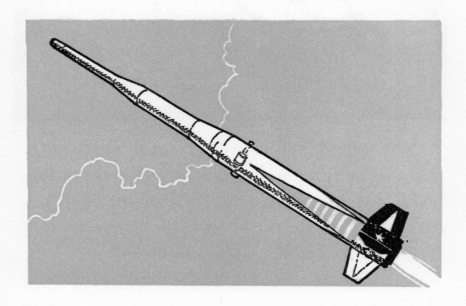

The X-17, built for the U. S. Air Force, is a "re-entry missile."

It is known by this name because the X-17 was built to find out what would happen when a rocket "re-entered" our atmosphere from space.

There were quite a number of difficulties.

The rocket had to throw out a nose cone that would re-enter the atmosphere. But it could not re-enter a long distance away from the take-off point because the scientists wanted to observe it. The next problem was that something that had been thrown to a height of, say, 200 miles would not normally fall back as fast as the scientists wanted it to.

What they wanted was what is called a "burn-up." They wanted the re-entering object to move so fast that it would be heated by friction against the atmosphere. In fact, they wanted it to heat up so much that the metal would melt and even become vapor. Once they succeeded in doing that, they could look around for materials which might resist such a burn-up. There are substances, called ceramics, which can stand much higher temperatures than metals.

So the problem was to produce a very high speed of re-entry in order to achieve a burn-up, but to do it above the proving ground from which the rocket was fired.

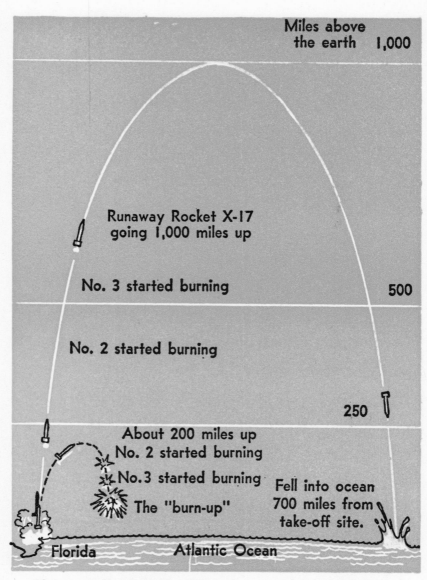

Miles above
the earth   1,000

Runaway Rocket X-17
going 1,000 miles up

No. 3 started burning   500

No. 2 started burning

250

About 200 miles up
No. 2 started burning
No. 3 started burning
The "burn-up"   Fell into ocean
                             700 miles from
                             take-off site.

Florida   Atlantic Ocean

The second and third rockets of one runaway X-17 began
burning before they started back to earth. The top
rocket climbed to 1,000 miles.

This is how they did it.

They put three rockets on top of each other. The first of these rockets took off at an angle of 80 degrees and threw the other two into space, to a height of about 200 miles. Then, on the way down, the second of these rockets started to burn. It burned in an upside down position to increase its speed. As soon as No. 2 had stopped burning, No. 3 began. It also pushed down, as fast as it could go.

The scientists got the "burn-up" they had been looking for. But early in 1957 one of the X-17s ran away. The second rocket did not wait until it was on the way down. It began burning as soon as it was free of No. 1. And No. 3 also burned as soon as it was free of No. 2. They all worked on the way up.

And the top rocket of this X-17 climbed to 1,000 miles!

10

The Buzz Bomb and Its Cousins

While the German army was working on the V-2 rocket during World War II, the German air force was working on another missile which was not a rocket. It was a new kind of weapon which might be called a pilotless airplane. It went by the name of V-1.

A V-1 looked like this from the outside:

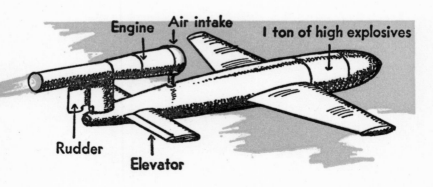

Engine Air intake 1 ton of high explosives

Rudder Elevator

The lower part, shaped like a torpedo, holds the war head, the fuel supply and the instruments that control the V-1. The part above, which looks like a stovepipe, is the engine.

The V-1 was also called the *buzz bomb*. It was really a small airplane without a pilot. It did not fly nearly as fast as a V-2. It could not be steered by radio messages once it started. But it was much simpler to build than the V-2 and much cheaper. And like the V-2, it could carry a ton of explosives.

The firing chamber of a V-1 looks like this inside:

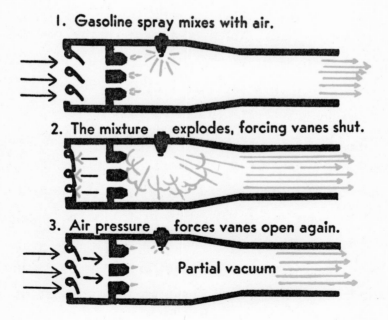

1. Gasoline spray mixes with air.

2. The mixture explodes, forcing vanes shut.

3. Air pressure forces vanes open again.

Partial vacuum

At the front you will see something like shutters, or the Venetian blinds on a window. This is just what they are. When they are closed, gasoline is sprayed into the firing chamber and set on fire by a spark plug like that in an automobile. It burns so fast that there is almost an explosion. The jet rushes out the rear end of the firing chamber and drives the V-1 forward.

Strong springs hold the shutters closed. But after the fuel explodes and the jet rushes out the rear, the pressure of air on the shutters is more than the springs can stand. They open again, and air rushes into the firing chamber. When this happens, the springs close the shutters again. At the same time more gasoline is sprayed into the firing chamber. The spark plug makes another spark, and there is another explosion.

This happens several times in a second—*boom, boom, boom*. The explosions come so fast that the V-1 sounds like a huge bee.

Because the explosions come like the beating of the pulse in your wrist, this type of engine is called the *pulse-jet*.

The trouble with a pulse-jet engine is in getting it started. Until it is going very fast, the pressure of the

The V-1 was fired from a launching ramp in the woods.

air in front is not enough to open the shutters. To get over this the Germans designed a special launching ramp which was built to point at the target city (London).

Along the center of the launching ramp, there was a strong metal tube with a piston in it. The tube was slotted and a kind of hook came out from the piston to hook into the V-1. The piston was driven by a hydrogen-peroxide container; when the V-1 reached the end of the ramp it moved fast enough for the pulse-jet to work.

A simple mechanical pilot kept the V-1 on a straight-line course. It also kept it at the altitude for which it had been "set." This was usually 2,000 feet. A few V-1s carried radios sending out signals. These were received by two or three German stations which drew lines to the place where the radio signal came from, as shown in this picture:

In that way they could tell how far this V-1 missile had traveled.

The V-1 usually traveled a distance of 150 miles. Its flying speed was 360 miles per hour. Since the English had some fighter planes that could fly a bit faster, these fighters could easily shoot down V-1s. The V-1s had no pilots, so of course they could not shoot back.

Many more V-1s were shot down by anti-aircraft guns controlled by radar. Near the end of the V-1 attack on London, only three out of every ten V-1s could get through the defenses. They did a great deal of damage but not enough to stop the British from continuing the war.

After the war American engineers tried to build a weapon like the V-1. The first one they finished was the U. S. Navy's Loon. The Loon needed only a very short ramp, no longer than its own length. The missile was attached to a piece of metal shaped like the letter T.

The rack drops away when the Loon is going fast enough to fly by itself.

The bottom of the T pointed forward. Along the crossbar there were four Jato units which burned together and threw the Loon into the air. When the four Jato units were used up, the T-shaped support dropped off. Such Loons were fired from a surfaced submarine.

The Loon was discontinued because the pulse-jet engine did not produce very high speeds. As long as all the manned airplanes were powered with piston engines and propellers, the pulse-jet propelled missiles could be faster. But when more and more jet planes, propelled by turbo-jet engines (see next chapter) were built, the piloted planes could always outfly the pulse-jet missiles.

There was only one thing to do, and that was to propel the missiles by turbo-jets too. Such turbo-jet engines are much more expensive than pulse-jets, but that could not be helped.

One of the turbo-jet propelled missiles has already been mentioned, the Matador. Another one much bigger than the Matador and with a range of over 4,500 miles is the Snark. One can start a turbo-jet engine with an electric starting motor, like that used in cars, but more powerful. But Jato units are used just the same to get the missile into the air faster.

The Snark

When a Snark is test-flown, it has two devices which it would not have when used as a missile. It has a device which turns it around after it has flown 2,000 miles. It then flies back to the proving ground where it came from. The other device is a landing gear. With the aid of commands transmitted by radio, the Snark can be landed on a runway, even though there is nobody in it. The same Snark can be test-flown several times by this method, saving expenses.

11

Turbo-Jets

There are several kinds of jet engines. They are all alike in that they produce an exhaust like a rocket that drives the plane forward. They are also alike in that they take from the air the oxygen for burning their fuel.

One of these jet engines has already been described, the pulse-jet. The other two kinds are called ram-jet and turbo-jet. The turbo-jet, which is the most common jet engine, was invented during World War II. In fact it was invented twice—in England by Commodore Whittle and in Germany by the engineers of the Heinkel Aircraft Company. They all wanted something that would make an airplane go very fast. Rockets started too fast. The hydrogen-peroxide rocket was about the right speed, but it could not stay up long. The pulse-jet is not very good for an airplane because it cannot be turned off and on again.

But a turbo-jet meets all these objections. At the front of a turbo-jet engine is a turbine with its blades set at an angle.

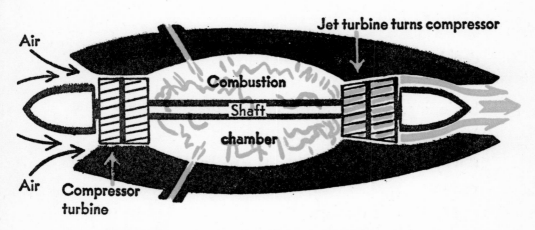

A turbo-jet moves faster and faster as the air is compressed.

This turbine whirls round and round. As it turns, it squeezes or compresses the air that comes in the front. This air furnishes the oxygen for burning the fuel in the firing chamber just behind the turbine.

As the air is compressed, it contains a great deal of

oxygen and will burn a lot of fuel at one time. The more fuel that is burned, the more power the engine gives.

Fuel is sprayed into the firing chamber and burns all the time, not in a series of explosions, as in the pulse-jet. At the rear end of the firing chamber there is another, smaller turbine. This takes a little of the power from the jet to turn the turbine that does the compressing. Connected with the compressor is a machine which finds out how much air is coming in. This decides how much fuel will be sprayed in.

A turbo-jet plane starts slowly because, at the beginning, the air is hardly compressed at all. Once it starts moving, it keeps going faster and faster. If it starts from the ground, it needs a long concrete runway.

On aircraft carriers, turbo-jet planes had to be shot into the air by means of catapults or had to take off with the help of Jato units. Though catapults and Jato units are still used, there are now jet planes which can take off without such help.

All jet engines use up fuel very fast. But they do not need the highly refined aviation gasoline that was necessary for propeller aircraft. They run on special

A Chance-Vought Cutlass catapults from a carrier deck.

jet fuels which are much cheaper than aviation gasoline. And because they fly so fast, the jet planes often fly more miles per gallon of fuel than propeller aircraft. Unfortunately jet engines are still far more noisy than other engines, but engineers hope to cure this.

Turbo-jet planes are much faster than planes with gasoline engines. They often go 600 miles an hour or more. They can also climb much higher than other planes. The trouble in getting other planes very high up is that the air is thin and it is hard to get enough oxygen for their engines. But a turbo-jet has its compressor. If the air is thin, the compressor works faster and the engine gets enough oxygen. Turbo-jets usually fly high up where they can make more speed.

But turbo-jets have their problems, too. One of them is that their cabins have to be entirely closed in and airtight. Up where they fly there would not be enough air for the pilot and passengers to breathe. They have to carry their own air with them, like a submarine under water. If something tears a hole in the cabin, it is just as bad as though there were a hole in the side of a submarine, only the air rushes out instead of the water rushing in.

Another problem of turbo-jets you can see for yourself by looking at a plane with this kind of engine. On most of the big ones, with four engines, you will see that the engines are out on long arms, away from the wings. On the small fighters you will see two big bulges at the ends of the wings.

U.S.A.F. F-89D Scorpion

The reason for both is the same. While a turbo-jet engine is running, it is very hot. The fuel tanks have to be placed a long way from the engines to keep the fuel from blowing up as a result of the heat. In the four-engined planes the fuel tanks are in the wings, and the engines are moved out from them. In the fighters the bulbs at the end of the wings hold the fuel tanks.

In other types of fighters, the engine is at the very tail. The air comes in at the front of the plane and

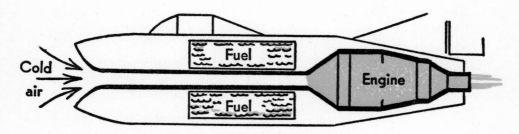

On certain types of fighters, cold air coming in at the front of the plane cools the fuel tanks on its way to the engine.

runs down a tube to reach the engine. As this air is quite cold when it goes past the fuel tanks in the middle of the plane, it helps to keep them cool and safe.

The heavier a turbo-jet plane is, the longer it has to run across the ground before getting into the air. Even a turbo-jet fighter plane needs a runway like a concrete street almost a mile long. Men quickly began to think about building big turbo-jet planes that would carry many people long distances, but it was quite clear that something would have to be done about getting them off the ground faster. A plane that had to run three or four miles before it could fly would not be very useful.

So a new type of engine was designed, called the jet-prop, now usually called a turbo-prop. A turbo-prop engine is exactly like a turbo-jet engine, with a compressor at the front and a turbine at the back to make the compressor work. But this turbine is bigger than the one in a turbo-jet engine. It takes more power from the jet. This extra power is used to turn a propeller.

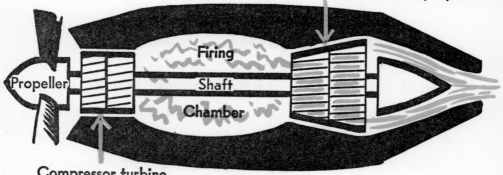

Jet turbine drives compressor and propeller

Propeller

Firing

Shaft

Chamber

Compressor turbine

In a jet-prop, or turbo-prop, engine, the turbine is larger and takes more power from the jet. This extra power turns the propeller.

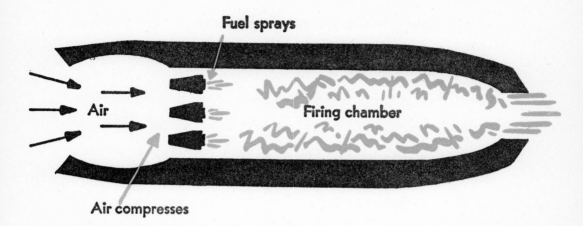

Fuel sprays

Air

Firing chamber

Air compresses

The ram-jet engine has no moving parts at all.

A turbo-prop engine gets a little more than half its push from the propeller. It may seem like a roundabout way of doing things to hire a jet to work a propeller, but a plane with turbo-prop engines can take off more easily and smoothly than one with turbo-jets. Pilots also like them because they are easy to land. It is hard to land a turbo-jet because the engine has to be going quite fast or not at all. The biggest planes with jet engines are mostly turbo-props.

Still another type of jet is called the *ram-jet* or *athodyd*. This is a strange jet engine which has no moving parts at all. Toward the front of the firing chamber is a row of nozzles which spray in the fuel.

With these nozzles are tubes, growing smaller toward the rear.

When a ram-jet is pushed rapidly through the air, air rushes in the front end. The tapered holes compress it, and this furnishes oxygen to burn the fuel. The jet rushes out the back, exactly as in a rocket, and pushes forward the engine and whatever goes with it. The ram-jet is really a kind of liquid-fuel rocket which gets its oxygen from the air. The faster it goes, the more air comes in. It can then burn more fuel. Engineers say of the ram-jet, "The faster it goes, the faster it goes." And this is quite true.

The ram-jet is so simple that it may seem surprising it is not used for everything. But the ram-jet is not quite so good as it looks. If such an engine is in a plane standing on the ground and fuel is sprayed into it and lighted, the plane simply stands still. There is not enough air in the firing chamber to burn up the fuel that would be needed to push the plane forward.

For a long time engineers were puzzled by the ram-jet. They knew it ought to work if they could find any way of getting it started. Finally, they built a ram-jet plane and took it up, attached to another very fast plane. When the other plane, called the "mother," was going over 400 miles an hour, the pilot of the ram-jet turned on his engine. It worked and his plane turned out to be faster than any other kind of jet plane.

Still, it is not very practical to send up two planes to get one of them started. There are not likely to be many planes with nothing but ram-jet engines.

However, the ram-jet can still be a great help to turbo-jet planes and often is. As you have seen, one of the great problems with turbo-jet planes is that the engine grows so very hot. Inside the engine there is so much of this heat that ordinary steel becomes as soft as butter and is not much use. The blades of the compressor have to be made of special metals. Even when such metals are used, it becomes important to get the burning gases out of the engine before they burn up the engine itself.

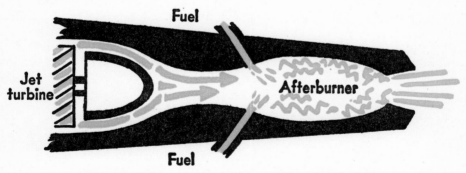

In this double engine, the ram-jet takes only gases from the turbo-jet at the left.

But this is wasteful, because those burning gases could still do some work. Mixed with them there is some oxygen that has not yet been used up. So the engineers thought of the idea of putting a ram-jet engine behind a turbo-jet and spraying more fuel into it.

In this double engine, the ram-jet does not take in air. It takes in only the gases coming from the turbo-jet. This is called *afterburning*. Most of the planes that can go faster than 700 miles an hour have these double engines with turbo-jets and ram-jets.

It used to be thought that when a plane reached the speed of sound, the sound waves would shake the plane to pieces. So the speed of 740 miles an hour, which is the speed of sound, was called the *sound barrier*. But when pilots reached this speed, nothing in particular happened. It was almost a disappointment.

12

Rockets at Work

Rockets can explore the upper atmosphere.

Rockets can put an artificial satellite into space and make it go around the earth. We shall talk more about this later.

In time, rockets will put a manned ship into such a satellite orbit, and similar rockets will probably be used to carry passengers over long distances on the earth. In the same way, missiles like the Snark might easily be used for the fast pilotless transportation of important letters and parcels.

Rockets can also go to the moon. But in order to understand how this can be done, we have to talk about something else first.

A single rocket could not be fast enough. We know exactly how fast a rocket would have to move in order to leave the earth. It would have to travel at a little more than seven miles a second. This is 420 miles a minute or 25,200 miles an hour.

Now the speed of a rocket depends on the speed with which the burning gases rush out from the firing chamber. This speed is called the *exhaust velocity*. The exhaust velocity of any combination that will burn can be calculated. There just isn't anything that will give a speed of 25,200 miles an hour.

Does this mean we have to give up? No. We have seen how modern American war rockets carry boosters

In a two-step rocket, both steps are real rockets. When the first drops away, the second starts firing at that speed.

to give them a start. The booster drops away when the rocket really begins to take hold and it is already moving very fast.

During the war, the Germans had an idea like this. They intended to shoot rockets like V-2s all the way across the Atlantic. Since a V-2 would not fly that distance by itself, they designed another, very big rocket to carry the V-2. It was called the A-10. The war head, or load of the A-10, was to have been a V-2. The Germans never finished the A-10, but there is nothing wrong with the idea. It is called a *two-step rocket*, and it is something quite different from a rocket with a booster.

A booster is something that merely gets a rocket off the ground. In a two-step rocket, both steps are real rockets, in business for themselves.

Suppose the first step of a two-step rocket is something like a V-2 and is making about 3,000 miles an hour. Just at this moment the first step drops away, and the second step starts firing. Now if this second step were fired from the ground, it would reach a speed of 3,000 miles an hour. But it is not being fired from the ground. It is being fired from something already going 3,000 miles an hour. Any speed it makes will be added

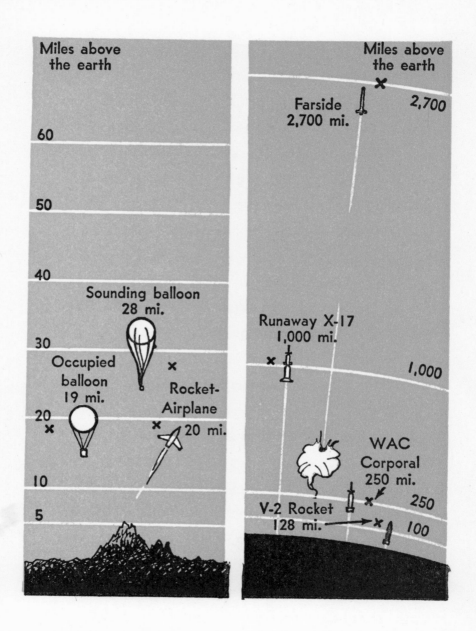

Miles above
the earth

60

50

40

Sounding balloon
28 mi.

30

Occupied
balloon
19 mi.

20

Rocket-
Airplane

x

x 20 mi.

10

5

Miles above
the earth

Farside
2,700 mi.

x

2,700

Runaway X-17
1,000 mi.

x

1,000

WAC
Corporal
250 mi.

V-2 Rocket
128 mi.

x

250

x

100

Each balloon, plane and rocket shown above set a new record.

to this 3,000 miles an hour, and it will soon be going twice as fast.

To see just how this would work out if it were really done, the U. S. Army asked the General Electric Company to build a two-step rocket. This was back in 1948, long before anybody thought of the X-17.

But the rockets to be used for the experiment—which was called Project Bumper—were not to be built just for this purpose. The engineers were told to work with rockets that were on hand.

There were quite a number of German V-2 rockets on hand. At the end of World War II, American soldiers had cleaned out the factory where the Germans had built their V-2s, and all of the rocket parts had been shipped to the United States. There were enough parts to assemble about 80 V-2 rockets. The German designers had been brought over, too, and helped.

A smaller rocket called the WAC Corporal had been built earlier in California. It was not the same as the Corporal missile mentioned in Chapter 9. It was a much smaller rocket weighing only about 700 pounds, and it could be fitted nicely into the nose of the V-2. So a V-2 was used as the first or lower step of the new rocket, and a WAC Corporal was used as the second step.

On February 24, 1949, the first two-stage liquid-fuel rocket in history was ready for firing at the White Sands Proving Ground in New Mexico.

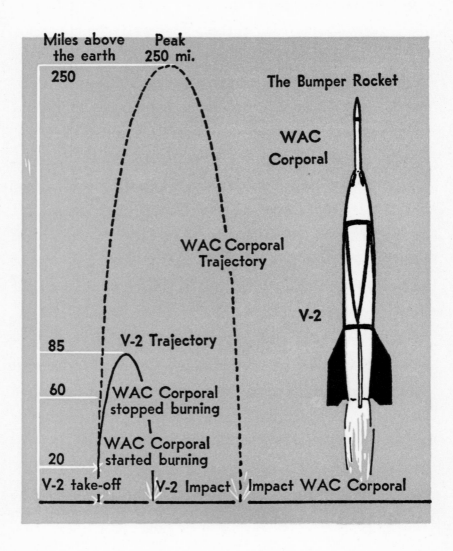

The V-2 took off as usual. Some 65 seconds after the firing, it had risen 20 miles. It also had used up its fuel. But it was moving upward at the rate of very nearly one mile per second.

Then the WAC Corporal was ignited. The small rocket could not produce a speed of a mile per second like the much bigger V-2. But it could produce a speed of four-tenths of a mile per second. With the added propulsion of the V-2, it was moving at 1.4 miles per second when it was about 60 miles above the ground. Then its fuel was gone. But it coasted to a height of 250 miles. For many years this was the high altitude record for rockets of any kind.

You may wonder why the WAC Corporal was ignited when only 20 miles up. Why didn't they wait until it had been carried by the V-2 to about 80 miles? The V-2 did coast that high.

The answer is that it was speed that counted, not height. The WAC Corporal, if fired by itself without any booster would probably have climbed to 30 miles. Therefore, if the experimenters had waited until the V-2 rocket had coasted to its 80-mile limit, the WAC Corporal could have added only 30 miles of altitude. That would have brought it no higher than 110 miles. Some V-2s have gone that high all by themselves.

THE WAC Corporal had to start burning while the V-2 was traveling at its fastest speed. This is the general rule for all rockets with more than one step. The second step should start when the first step has reached its greatest speed, no matter how high it is at the moment.

But this rule is true only if the rocket is higher than 20 miles in the atmosphere. Below 20 miles it can be harmful to be too fast. The air is too dense and causes loss of speed. This is illustrated by the "Rockoon."

This Rockoon is a Deacon rocket combined with a Skyhook balloon.

Several years ago the armed services had a new solid-fuel rocket which was named the Deacon. The Deacon rocket· was not very large, but if it was fired from the ground it could coast up to a height of 60,000 feet. The Deacon was large enough to carry a few scientific instruments.

Then one scientist reasoned that the Deacon probably would go much higher than 60,000 feet if it did not try to go through the dense air so fast. Of course the Deacon could have had a liquid-fuel first stage. Though liquid-fuel rockets can be faster than solid-fuel rockets, they take their time building up speed. For this reason they go through the densest air near the ground comparatively slowly.

This could have been done, but the Deacon was to be fired from a fairly small ship. The ship did not have room for large liquid-fuel rockets. Nor did it have tanks for rocket fuels. It also did not have the firing platform such a rocket needs. So the scientist reasoned that he could lift the Deacon with a balloon. He used a so-called Skyhook balloon, which is made of very thin plastic, to lift the rocket to 60,000 feet. When the ballon hovered at that altitude, the Deacon was fired. It climbed to 55 miles.

In the case of the Rockoon—the word was put together from the two words "rocket" and "balloon"—the balloon provided no speed at all. It just provided a means of lifting the rocket above the densest layers of the atmosphere.

Scientists then knew that they had understood the problem correctly. If a rocket builds up its speed slowly, like a liquid-fuel rocket, it can be fired from the ground without losing much altitude due to air resistance. But if the rocket builds up a high speed in a few seconds, as a solid-fuel rocket will, it should be lifted into thin layers of the air before the solid fuel is ignited.

This idea was carried out again in 1957 with another rocket which was called Project Farside. Project Farside was a four-stage rocket, all four stages solid fuel. Its top stage would build up to a very high velocity very fast. Therefore it needed a balloon lift.

The balloon was again a plastic Skyhook balloon. The four-stage rocket dangled from it, its nose pointing into a round opening at the bottom of the balloon. A balloon can be open at the bottom; no gas will escape since the gas is in its upper half. When the balloon was 80,000 feet up, the rocket was fired. It went through the balloon, which then fell into the Pacific Ocean

The four-stage Project Farside needed a balloon lift.

underneath. All four stages burned in quick succession, and the top stage climbed to 2,700 miles.

That is, we *know* that it went that high. But it may have gone a few hundred miles higher. At a height of 2,700 miles, the radio transmitter stopped. But the rocket was probably still moving and may have gone to 3,000 miles.

About a year before the rocket combination called Project Farside was carried to Eniwetok Island in the Pacific Ocean, another big shot had been made across the Atlantic Ocean.

This was the first shot of a step rocket now well known under the name of Jupiter C. The date was September 20, 1956. The place was the missile test center at Cape Canaveral in Florida. The rocket was what rocket engineers call a "mixed job." This term means that some of the stages of the rocket burned liquid fuel while others used a solid fuel.

The Jupiter C rocket had three stages. The first stage was a liquid-fuel rocket. The second stage had solid fuel, but it was not just one rocket. It was a

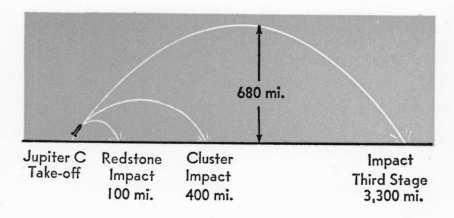

Jupiter C
Take-off

Redstone
Impact
100 mi.

Cluster
Impact
400 mi.

680 mi.

Impact
Third Stage
3,300 mi.

so-called "cluster." This means that several, say six, solid-fuel rockets of the same size and type are bundled together. The type of solid-fuel rocket used is called Recruit, because it is a smaller edition of a solid-fuel rocket called Sergeant. The third stage was a single Recruit rocket.

This Jupiter C rocket was fired to reach a great distance, not to go to a great height. The first stage, the liquid-fuel stage, fell into the ocean 100 miles from the missile test center. The second stage, the cluster of solid-fuel rockets, fell into the ocean about 400 miles from the test center. And the third stage traveled to a point 3,300 miles away. But in going to a distance of 3,300 miles, it climbed 680 miles high.

13

Rockets in Space

In the course of a few years, as you have read in the earlier chapters of this book, several rockets had gone into space. These included the WAC Corporal of Project Bumper, the "run-away" X-17 and the top stage of the Jupiter C. And, of course, there was Project Farside.

But for years scientists had known that shooting higher and higher was not really enough. If a rocket is shot vertically into and through the atmosphere, it is bound to fall back every time. However, it won't fall back if it can be made to travel at the rate of 7 miles per second or 25,200 miles per hour.

A rocket going upward at this rate will go all the way to the moon. It will be too fast for earth's gravity to pull it back. It will, so to speak, escape from the earth's gravity. For this reason the velocity of 7 miles per second is called the *escape velocity*.

Scientists had been quite willing, of course, to try for a rocket with escape velocity. But they were sure that even before they built one with escape velocity, they could put a rocket into space in such a manner that it would circle the earth. In other words they could make an artificial satellite.

This needs less velocity than escaping from the earth. If one could put an artificial satellite a few hundred feet up, it would need 5 miles per second or 18,000 miles per hour. Of course one cannot put a satellite a few hundred feet up. Or a few thousand feet. There is far too much air resistance. It simply would not work.

But the scientists were sure an artificial satellite could be put into an orbit around the earth at a height where there is no atmosphere any more. It could be done at a height of, say 200 or 300 miles. At that height it would not have to go at 5 miles per second. It would need less, about 4.6 miles per second, or about 16,500 miles per hour. This could be done with a three-stage rocket.

It would be best, the scientists said, if the first and second stages of this rocket burned liquid fuels. The third stage could be a solid-fuel rocket.

In 1955 the United States announced that it would shoot an artificial satellite into an orbit. In 1956 the Russians said they would do it too. Both countries said that they would shoot several such artificial satellites between July, 1957, and December, 1958. The reason for picking this time was that these eighteen months had been chosen as the "International Geophysical Year." Sixty-four different nations, working together,

The black line shows the artificial satellite in orbit around the earth. The colored line shows orbit above equator.

were to explore the earth during this "year." Exploring nearby space was considered part of the job of exploring the earth. That's why both the United States and Russia prepared artificial satellites.

The Russians shot first on October 4, 1957, and they called their artificial satellite *sputnik*. This is a Russian word meaning a person, or a thing, with whom or with which you travel. It can be a friend, or it can be something you always have along on your trips, like an alarm clock. Because the word sputnik can have so many meanings, the Russians did not call their first satellite sputnik only. They called it *sputnik zemli* which means "companion of earth."

Sputnik No. 1 as it was soon called needed ninety-six minutes to go around the earth once. Its orbit was not a circle but a figure which is called an ellipse. When sputnik No. 1 was closest to the ground, it was 156 miles up. When farthest from the ground it was 560 miles up. Astronomers have special terms for these two points. The point closest to the ground is called the *perigee*. The one which is farthest away is called the *apogee*.

Sputnik No. 2 was fired by the Russians on November 3, 1957. Its elliptical orbit was ten miles lower at perigee and almost 1,100 miles from the ground at apogee. In both cases that point nearest the ground, the perigee, was still in the upper atmosphere.

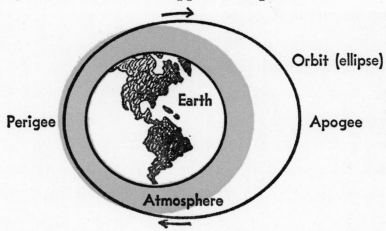

The third artificial satellite to be put into an orbit around the earth was American. It was fired from Cape Canaveral on January 31, 1958, one hour and twelve minutes before midnight. The rocket used to put it into orbit was a modified Jupiter C which consisted of a total of four steps. The first stage was a liquid-fuel rocket resembling the Redstone. The other three stages were solid-fuel rockets. The first American satellite, named Explorer, weighed about 31 pounds. Its orbit was larger than that of either of the two Russian satellites. The perigee of Explorer was 219 miles from the ground, the apogee 1600 miles.

What keeps these satellites up in space? The earth's gravity is responsible. This picture will explain it.

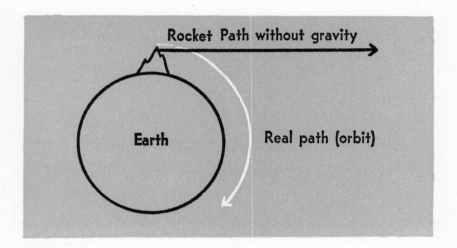

If you fired a fast rocket parallel to the ground, it would go away in a straight line if there were no gravity. But there is gravity. If the velocity is just right—4.6 miles per second, as mentioned—gravity bends the line into a closed orbit.

If the orbit is far enough from the earth—that is, outside the atmosphere—the satellite would go on forever. There is nothing to stop it. It might be hit every once in a while by a tiny meteor. But these meteors are as small as dust grains. They would not stop the satellite.

But nobody wants the first satellites to stay in space forever. For this reason, they are shot in such a manner that the perigee end of the orbit is still in the upper atmosphere. Every time it goes through that portion of its orbit, the air gets in its way.

This makes the whole orbit shrink.

Now look back at the picture on page 128.

If you imagine that the orbit shrinks, you will see that more and more of it will come within the atmosphere. As time goes on, the satellite will be going through more air each time it circles the earth. In the end, most of the orbit will be inside the atmosphere. Then the satellite will not go out into space any more. Battered by the air, it will break up. The pieces will then fall. They won't fall straight down but at a slant. But they will fall and, in falling, burn up.

Then the sky will be clear again.

But why did the scientists want to shoot such artificial satellites?

The reason is the same as for any other experiment: to learn something. The scientists wanted to know how much air is left at a height of 150 miles. They wanted to know how much a satellite in space is heated by the sun; how much it cools off in the earth's shadow.

Scientists have to know these things and many others before the next step can be taken. That next step is to put a man into an orbit around the earth.

Of course the ship in which a man goes into an orbit will not look like the small artificial satellites. It will not be ball-shaped and it will not even be rocket-shaped. The man will have to come back and eventually he will have to land. For this reason his ship must have wings.

The wings will not be needed for the take-off, and they will be completely useless in space. But they are needed for landing on the earth. The ship will probably look like the modern fighter planes do. It will have triangular wings; *delta wings* is the name for them.

The first piloted ship will not stay in orbit for weeks or even months like an artificial satellite. It will go into an orbit, stay there for twenty-four hours, and then the pilot will return. He will not have to wait for his orbit to shrink. He will be able to break out of the orbit at any time and go back into the atmosphere. He will have a fuel reserve for this purpose.

The pilot will not even have to do much observing. The instruments in the ship will do that for him. They will broadcast their findings to the ground and tape record them too. In that way the scientists on the ground will be able to go over the findings again and again.

After a few such flights have been made, the next step will be the establishment of a manned space station. This space station will be a large artificial satellite. It will be in an orbit which does not touch the atmosphere. And it very likely will be 1,075 miles up. In such an orbit it will need precisely two hours to go around the earth.

The manned space station will be built in an orbit around the earth, 1,075 miles from the ground.

The space station will be put together on the ground. It will be much too heavy to be carried by a single rocket ship, and it will have a shape that cannot be pushed through the air at a high speed. So it will have to be taken apart, and the pieces will be loaded into transport rockets.

It may take twenty or thirty flights to get all the pieces into the orbit. As they are brought up, they will be put together again.

Such a station would have many uses.

It would give a better view of the stars than anyone has ever had before. Living at the bottom of the ocean of air, we never get a really good view. Our atmosphere is in the way. This is partly because water droplets and dust particles float in it, but mostly because the air is never really still. Looking into the sky through a telescope is very often like looking at the bottom of a brook through its moving water.

The space station would also be very useful for helping to predict the weather. Our weathermen on the ground never know much about the weather beyond the shoreline. They never know what the weather is like in the Arctic. But storms may develop over the ocean, or in the Arctic, before they get to us.

The space station can also keep a watch on icebergs drifting in the oceans and radio warnings to ships. It could even find a ship which drifted off after a storm, disabled, and direct rescue forces to it. You can see how many uses a space station will have.

Since the space station will be like an island outpost in the ocean, everything the men need will have to be brought up by transport rockets. But they will not require as much as one might think. A man needs about three pounds of oxygen per day to breathe. He would need more if he were doing heavy work. But the men in the space station will not do heavy work. They will take pictures, look at picture screens, make radio telephone calls and perform other similar duties.

A man needs about four pounds of liquid to drink per day. And he eats about three and a half pounds of food daily. This, combined with 3 pounds of oxygen, totals 10½ pounds per day per man. Let us be generous and allow 12 pounds per man per day. If there are thirty men in the space station they need 360 pounds of oxygen, food and drink to stay alive. For one day, that is. For one week they would need 2,520 pounds. For two weeks they would need a little over 5,000 pounds. And for a whole month about 10,000 pounds or about five tons. The ships which build the space station can easily carry twice as much.

The space station could be supplied with just one flight every month. And when the space station is finished and working, engineers will begin to plan for the next steps.

These will be flights to the moon and to other planets. Scientists already know the questions they hope to have answered by such flights, and engineers have ideas of how it could be done. But they cannot really work on these problems until they have the space station. It is for this reason that the space station has been called "the door to the universe."

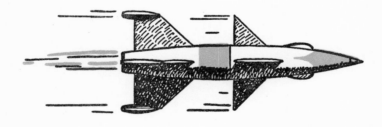

Index

Index

Index

Index

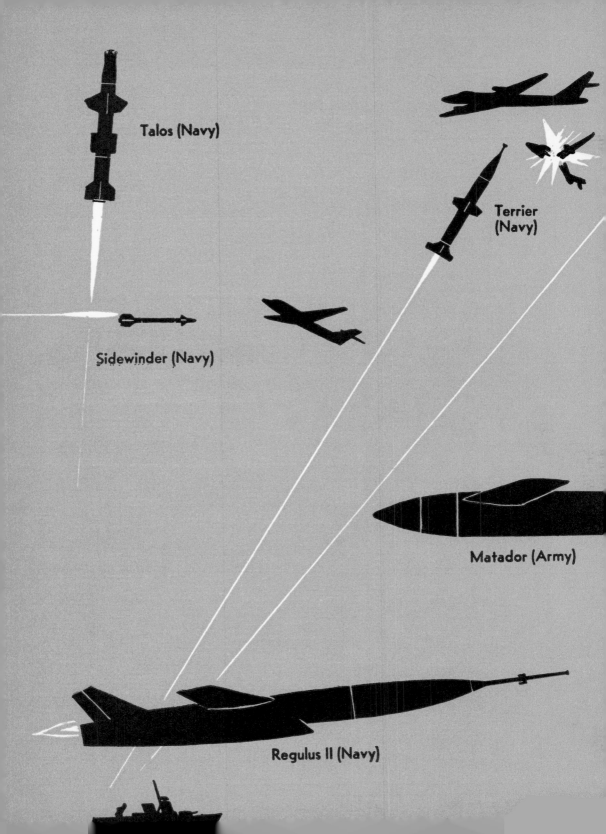

Talos (Navy)

Terrier (Navy)

Sidewinder (Navy)

Matador (Army)

Regulus II (Navy)